BELIEFS, PRINCIPLES & PRACTICES

A Collection of ELT Articles

***

Vicky Saumell

This book is dedicated to two people who changed my professional life.

Alex Campo, my best teacher ever, who selflessly shared her immense language knowledge with me and taught me to love the English language.

And **Susan Hillyard**, who convinced me that I should start sharing my experience with other teacher and set me on the path to become a conference presenter and trainer.

I am forever grateful for their friendship and mentoring.

Table of Contents

Part 3: Integrating technology

Introduction

You might be wondering why I have decided to publish this book. I noticed that my writing was scattered all over the web and print. And when I went back to it, I saw it was quite a body of information and opinion about my teaching experience. So I collected all my articles and pieces of writing and re-organised them into this collection. It is meant to be a starting point for discussion and reflection about my favourite ELT topics. You might notice that some ideas appear over and over in different articles, because they reflect my teaching and learning beliefs, principles and practices, and therefore, they transpire my writing in general.

PART 1: Being a Teacher

My journey as a teacher: a winding road

Teachers often get asked how is it that they decided to be teachers, and I am no exception. My journey in the teaching career began when I was 18 years old and developed in two different areas at the same time over the years. I had just finished secondary school and I decided that I would study to become a PE teacher, which I did. But I also needed to work to help at home while I was studying and I was offered a job teaching English to young learners in the private language school where I had studied. I felt insecure about it at first but confident that I could learn on the job and become better. I had had a teacher, Alex Campo, who had been a role model to me and had indeed made me love the language! This went on for a few years until I graduated as a PE teacher. It was time to decide which area I wanted to focus on, English or PE? What had started as a temporary job was now something I really loved and did not want to leave behind. I decided to keep working part-time jobs in both areas and eventually the balance was tipped towards English. I enrolled in Translation Studies and have never stopped studying and learning about English since that first teaching job in 1986.

However, it wasn't till the late 90s that my perceptions as a teacher began to shift. I started to see myself as an agent of change in education. I got my first Coordination position in the secondary school where I was teaching (and still do!) and began to address a bigger picture than the classroom. I also became increasingly interested in technology and ways to use it in language learning. Technology helped me to connect with educators from other parts of the world and that literally changed my life as a teacher.

I also started feeling that I had lots of things I wanted to share with other teachers and with the invaluable help of my mentor, Susan

Hillyard, I started making my first steps into conference presentations and materials writing. Then came the opportunity to publish something I had written with a major publisher and the Latin American Scholarship to attend the IATEFL conference in 2010.

These two events opened many doors so that I could further develop professionally and contribute my own experiences to the ELT community. I have since spent my time teaching, reflecting on my teaching, training teachers, writing and presenting my ideas. All of this has been made possible by sharing and exchanging experiences with teachers worldwide. Becoming a connected teacher, through social media and face to face interactions, has allowed me to become more involved with teaching English and education in general and definitely more open-minded.

I am now in a position where I feel I have to give back some of the immense help, mentoring and consideration I received in the early years of my career by mentoring other teachers, helping out whenever I can, and doing volunteer work for teaching associations and others. Teaching English is my passion and almost 30 years after that first teaching job, I have no regrets whatsoever and I cannot possibly see myself doing anything else!

Teaching is such a rewarding profession! But it has so many facets worth exploring! If I could summarise it in few words, these would be: exploring, connecting, sharing, learning.

September 2015

Available online at http://www.teachingenglish.org.uk/blogs/vicky-saumell/vicky-saumell-my-journey-a-teacher-a-winding-road

Teacher development tips for novice teachers

Novice teachers fresh out of teacher training colleges or CELTA courses, for example, are usually anxious to get better at their craft but usually get lost in the routine of planning, teaching, marking, etc. These are a few simple ideas to keep up with teacher development.

Read, read, read

Keeping up to date with new trends in language teaching and learning is essential. What you studied during your teacher training time is very valuable but needs adjusting to new ideas, methods, approaches and theories all the time. Reading is a must. Whether it is books, journals, blog posts or any other kind of writing, reading about your areas of interest is a way of keeping updated.

Maximise staff room time

The Staff Room is a place that can become a wasted opportunity. Talk to other teachers about classes you share, strategies to deal with certain difficulties, successful tasks and projects. Ask for advice, plan joint projects with other teachers or classes. The Staff Room has the potential to be a great space for teacher development.

Connect with other teachers

A major source of new ideas are other teachers. You may already have a group of colleagues from the school you teach in or former trainees, with whom you communicate regularly. But what about a wider community of teachers from all over the world? Twitter and Facebook are just two examples of tools that can allow you to widen your circle.

Connecting with teachers all over the world can open the door to ideas exchange, collaboration and much more! If you are daunted by Twitter, you can start by joining #ELTchat on Wednesdays for a more focused experience.

Transfer and experiment

Do not just read and exchange ideas, put them into practice! Take in what might work and adapt it for your context. Do not be afraid of trying new things and sharing the experience with your colleagues everywhere. It is by daring into new paths that we can discover what works and what doesn't.

Share your knowledge

You may feel you have nothing to offer. However, do not be afraid to share your experiences, whether successful or not. There are lots of other teachers who could benefit from them. You can start local and try to set up a workshop in your school. If you are self- conscious about public speaking, you can start a blog to share your ideas. Every experienced speaker or writer, had to start once...

Becoming a teacher is only the beginning of a life-long learning career. Find time to explore your areas of interest and connect to like-minded professionals who can help you in your endeavour. After more than 25 years of teaching, I feel the most rewarding professional development opportunities have come from the personal and professional connections I have made over the years.

April 2014

Available online at http://www.teachingenglish.org.uk/blogs/vicky-saumell/teacher-development-tips-novice-teachers

Avoiding teacher burnout

I have been teaching English for more than 25 years and although there have been a few times when I felt exhausted and demotivated, I have always found a way to get my energy and motivation back. So here are a few suggestions that have worked out for me, in no particular order.

Fight routine

I think one of our main enemies is routine, so finding new ways of doing things and varying the things we do in and out of the classroom can be a way of winning the battle. Teaching different levels or age groups each semester or year will also keep you alert. Changing the materials you use is also revitalising. You may not be able to change everything as it may be imposed upon you, but you can always change the supplementary activities you do. Propose changes or new projects to your superiors; they will hopefully be open to new suggestions and ideas!

Find joy in teaching

If you love what you do, it's easier to stay motivated. Whenever you can choose, go for topics, methods, strategies that you enjoy.

Connect with other teachers

Connecting is a way of sharing your burdens, and your successes, with somebody else. They might feel the same and share strategies to help you overcome the burdens and rejoice in the successes. Build a network of teachers with whom you can share your experiences. Social media has made this possible very easily!

Choose an aspect of language teaching you enjoy and go further into it. Do a course. Read. Research. Find your niche!

Find something else you can do as a teacher

You may like writing; start a blog or try writing new materials. Start giving presentations locally. Join a teacher association and collaborate with the organisation. Do an action research project. Carry out a project with a twin class somewhere else.

Change your job

If you are not happy where you are working, try finding a different school or place to work as a teacher. Every school has a particular environment and culture that may not fit your style.

Use your free time wisely

Do things you really enjoy. Find the time to pursue a hobby or practise a sport or do an activity you've always wanted to do: cooking, pottery, even learning another language! Even if you love your job, you need to have a mental break from it.

Above all, remember you are not alone and you are not the only who feels this way. We have all felt it in different ways along our professional lives!

May 2014

Available online at http://www.teachingenglish.org.uk/blogs/vicky-saumell/vicky-saumell-avoiding-teacher-burnout

What makes an effective manager?

In my experience of both managing and being managed in multiple and varied situations, I have come to collect some useful tips, which I would love to share with you.

You may have the most wonderful group of teachers in your institution, but the difference between success and failure is a mindful guidance from the manager or coordinator to give your team a sense of common direction. So here it goes:

• Have a plan!

• Respect your teachers' individuality

• Promote and value teamwork

• Take advantage of your teachers' talents. Help them discover what they are and let them share what they do best so that the whole team can grow.

• Create opportunities for professional growth. Encourage your teachers to explore new paths, give talks, engage with teacher's associations, etc.

• Listen to your teachers! Listen to their concerns and help them to overcome them. Guide them in their own path to become better teachers. Celebrate their successes.

• Try to make decisions by reaching consensus. If this is not possible, clearly explain to your teachers the reasons behind your informed decisions.

• Be open to new ideas coming from your teachers.

• Within your guidance, allow teachers some choice in what to do or how to do it.

• In meetings, have clear objectives. Prepare an agenda and share it before the meeting. Set a starting and finishing time for the meeting and keep to it! Use time wisely, ask teachers to prepare for the meeting and do not use up time for things that can be debated in an email exchange or a Facebook discussion.

• Make sure you reward teachers. If meetings are not paid, bring something to eat, make coffee or give teachers a treat at the end. Thank them for their time and cooperation. Sincere acknowledgement works wonders! Sometimes, it does not take more than a personal note.

In a few words, an effective manager is knowledgeable, open-minded and human. They guide, facilitate, inspire, rather than tell you what to do. I wish I had had such a manager at times...

October 2016

Available online at http://www.teachingenglish.org.uk/blogs/vicky-saumell/vicky-saumell-what-makes-effective-manager

PART 2: Teaching and Learning

Coursebooks as guides

Language learning has long been dependent on the coursebook. And coursebooks have been the recipients of both praise and criticism. We probably need to look at the coursebook from a different perspective.

When the coursebook becomes the syllabus, we run the risk of becoming too tied up with its contents and probably oblivious of other important aspects that the coursebook may not address adequately.

Coursebook writers try to create their option of the best possible sequence of contents that follow a certain methodology or approach for a general audience. As teachers, we know that there are many different contexts in which coursebooks are used. These are related to cultural differences, teaching and learning beliefs, number of students, type of school, reason for learning the language, among others. It is practically impossible for a writer to come up with a one-size-fits-all solution embodied in a coursebook. And that is where teachers and administrators who believe the coursebook is there to be followed blindly, fail to acknowledge effective ways to maximize the potential of coursebooks.

When we understand that a coursebook is an ally instead of a master plan, we can start making choices that will result in more effective teaching and learning.

So here are some perceived disadvantages of coursebooks and my suggestions for overcoming them:

The topics are ok for my context, but the specific readings are not
> Find other readings that can relate more to your specific class and context. Find something more local.

The contents' sequence is not adequate for my context > Do not be afraid to change the sequence of the units or contents within a unit. Look for a more organic and meaningful order for your class.

The language presentation methodology is the traditional Presentation, Practice, Production > If you want to try an inductive approach to language presentation, look for a reading or listening text in the coursebook in which you can find the target structure and do that first to expose students to the language, then ask students some guiding questions to help them discover the rule by analysing the examples in the text, only then show them the language presentation section in the book and finally move on to the practice tasks. This approach is called Guided Discovery.

Some contents are developed superficially > Find extra material to supplement these contents.

There is too much emphasis on certain aspects and little on others > It may be that a coursebook is weak on pronunciation and intonation tasks, for example. Create a custom-made parallel thread to develop that aspect.

The suggested ideas for teaching in the teacher's book are not adequate for my context > Create your own learning paths for certain content: add warmers or icebreakers, skip other suggested tasks, make sure you personalize the learning experience.

There is no multimedia component > Look for videos to complement the topics in the coursebook.

Some readings present outdated information > Find updated readings or videos and have students compare what has changed.

There are no integration tasks to consolidate the learning > Create a custom-made project at the end of each unit which integrates the concepts and vocabulary and that fits your students interests and learning preferences.

If you have an option to choose your own coursebook, try a shorter coursebook that allows you to create a more personalised learning experience based on your learners' interests and preferences and according to your own objectives and beliefs as a teacher. Nobody knows your students better than you. Trust your intuition and knowledge! And remember we can probably have better experiences if we consider coursebooks as guides.

February 2014

Available online at http://www.teachingenglish.org.uk/blogs/vicky-saumell/vicky-saumell-coursebooks-guides

The role of methodologies and approaches in organic lessons

Almost any teaching handbook or course will include a detailed explanation of existing methodologies and approaches. And although knowing this is extremely important, it is naive to think that there is one perfect method that will solve all our teaching and learning problems.

Over the years, I have found that due to my own beliefs about the teaching and learning processes, I tend to favour certain strategies over others. However, I can say that my lessons usually include an eclectic mix. The question is "How does this mix come about?"

My current practice, after 25 years of experience, is a reflection of previous instances of trying things out and finding out what works best for me in certain scenarios. Therefore, I can choose to do Presentation, Practice and Production or Guided Discovery, depending on the target structure to be taught. I can also do Task Based Learning or Project Based Learning if the topic seems suitable. Dogme? Of course! And Communicative Language Teaching usually! I have also tried Test, Teach, Test, used translation strategies and compared L1 and L2 in monolingual classes. I also favour Teacher Talking Time sometimes if I feel my students may benefit from my telling them a story or experience.

In my early teaching years, I used to be much stricter about my lesson planning stage and the decisions I made while planning were seldom changed. Later, I started being more flexible and planned alternative paths to follow depending on how the actual class was going. These days, my plans are more of a loose guide that is filled up as the lesson progresses. I can do this because I am much more confident about reading and assessing the classroom situations and choosing what is best more spontaneously. This is possible because I have a solid knowledge base and a myriad of past experiences to back up my 'instincts'.

A final consideration. When trying to achieve a more spontaneous and organic lesson, it is essential to have a body of knowledge and experiences to fall back on, as well as to allow yourself to experiment with new options regularly in order to feed this bank of experiences. You could always do the same thing over and over but isn't variety the spice of life?

September 2016

Available online at http://www.teachingenglish.org.uk/blogs/vicky-saumell/vicky-saumell-role-methodologies-approaches-organic-lessons

Choice as an alternative to a negotiated syllabus

The idea of a negotiated syllabus has been around for quite a while and has been met with both praise and criticism. My personal reaction to it is that it can be applied in limited, very specific contexts where there is not a mandatory curriculum to be taught.

So I would like to focus on an alternative that can be useful in a much wider variety of contexts choice.

I am a fervent practitioner of offering my students choice whenever possible within a lesson. Offering choice does not mean walking into a classroom and asking students what they want to do. This would probably result in chaos. I mean choice as a planned strategy within a lesson. The way I see it, when I plan a lesson I have a main objective in mind, maybe more, that is not up for choice. However, there are different ways of achieving your aims and I like to be open to multiple possibilities and giving my students an opportunity to find their own paths.

Depending on your main objectives, you may be able to consider choice in the type of task to be carried out, the tools to be used, ways to present students' products, topic, etc.

• If the main aim is learning to write an argumentative essay or improving their presentation skills, the topic could be freely chosen.

• When doing grammar or vocabulary practice, you could come up with at least two different task types, or even have students create a practice task themselves, following a model task type directory. I first saw this idea of providing task type models in Cambridge English for

Schools and Cambridge English Worldwide by Andrew Littlejohn and Diana Hicks.

• For project presentations, students could choose the way to present them. An oral presentation, a slide presentation, a paper or digital poster, a video...

• If you want to improve reading, why not let them choose what to read with appropriate guidance for reading level? Surely, they will read more enthusiastically if it is something they like.

An important consideration for managing choice in the classroom is that some students may not be comfortable with the idea of unlimited choice. This may result in blank, paralyzed minds. A possible solution is having a list of alternatives for students to choose from, while still allowing more daring students to come up with ideas off the list.

Exercising choice usually results in students becoming more responsible for the tasks at hand, not to mention more student engagement and a perceived teacher's respect for their needs and interests.

September 2016

What are your top 5 tips for teaching teenagers?

Teenagers are often described as an unwelcome bunch of learners that pose multiple difficulties to teachers. And it may be true as it is for any age group when you do not know how to deal with them. I have been teaching teenagers for the past 20 years and they are in fact my favourite age group. So here are my top 5 tips for teaching teens.

Rapport: Building rapport with teens is essential for success. If you don't, they will probably complain about everything and anything you say or propose. A genuine interest in them and their lives will really improve your relationship with teenagers. They have a talent for seeing through you and knowing if you are being genuine or faking this interest. You could use the first minutes of class to engage in informal conversation about their lives.

Interests: Take time to get to know their interests and using them in your planning. You can do an online survey, for example with Survey Monkey, at the beginning of the year and then use the results to inform your planning. It's difficult to please everybody but you can go for popular topics chosen by many of your students. Even if your syllabus is constrained in terms of what you can add, you can organise reading, listening and speaking tasks around these topics of interest. You can also take into account their preferred type of activities: listening to music, watching whole films, watching short videos, etc., which will vary from group to group.

Choice: My favourite!!!!! Build choice into your classroom activities. I have experimented with different ways of introducing choice into my lessons. It should be clear that you cannot just let students choose what they want to do. I refer to choice as a planned strategy within a lesson. In order to do so, you first need to identify the main objective of your task. That is not up for choice! Once your main objective is clear you can come up with more than one way of achieving it. The choice can be in the type of task, the tool to be used, the way to present it, among others.

Here are some examples:

• If you want students to write a narrative or argumentative essay or any other type of text, you can provide a few alternative titles for them to choose.

• If you want to revise certain vocabulary or grammar, you can write at least two different task types for the same concept.

• If you want students to make a presentation on a specific topic, you can let students choose what tool to use to make the presentation. Powerpoint? A video? A poster? Let them choose!

• If you want students to improve their presentations skills and fluency, you can allow them to choose the topic. Let it be something they are interested in! (which links to the previous tip).

• If you have worked with a book and you want students to do a wrap-up project, you can let them come up with ideas of what to do. You can always guide them by giving them a few options so that they know what you expect from them. In this case it is a wise idea to approve the choices before any work is done in order to avoid misdirected tasks or projects.

You may be thinking that this implies more work for the teacher and although it is in some cases, the benefits in terms of motivation are far greater.

Variety: Teens get bored easily. Use variety as your ally. You can vary topics, types of tasks, etc. Predictability can ruin your class. You can change the order in which you normally do things and come up with unexpected, original tasks to break down classroom routine. If you have the possibility of changing where you can have your class, do so! A classroom, a library, a playground, a garden.... Anywhere is good for a lesson. You can plan for specific tasks to be done in these alternative spaces.

Challenge: Do not play it safe.... Add challenge. Challenge can come in different ways.

• Creating slightly more difficult tasks. More difficult tasks will require more concentration on the part of the learners and will stretch their minds thus increasing student engagement.

• Introducing competitions in the classroom. Most teens are very competitive and will get involved in almost any task if there is a competition element involved. Make sure you keep track of points and set up a prize system, maybe monthly.

• Going for open-ended tasks. You can provide multiple points of entry and allow for varied and multiple possible solutions. This is also related to choice and interests. It is also a way of personalising tasks. It will increase motivation and promote creativity.

If you have been assigned a group of teens, do not despair! Try these tips and experiment with your own ideas as well. Teens are as enjoyable as any other age group!

January 2014

Available online at http://www.teachingenglish.org.uk/blogs/vicky-saumell/what-are-your-top-5-tips-teaching-teenagers-vicky-saumell

CLIL and Cultural Diversity

A first look at CLIL will probably result in considerations about the content and the language to be taught, their relationship and different models of implementation. However, an essential aspect that is sometimes overlooked is culture. So what is the relationship between culture and CLIL? How do language, content and culture interact and affect each other? Before we can start looking into that, we need to clarify the term culture.

What's culture?

As most people do these days, I resorted to Wikipedia for a definition that would help me understand.

"The set of shared attitudes, values, goals, and practices that characterizes an institution, organization, or group"

Retrieved from Wikipedia

This definition still fails to make the connection clear, so I went a little further in my search for clarification and found that if we look into "culture" a bit deeper we can see that what we usually consider culture falls into one of these more easily observed aspects.

The **twelve aspects** of culture for grouping information when studying countries are:

1. Food

2. Clothing

3. Recreation

4. Government

5. Education

6. Language

7. Religion

8. Transportation

9. Economy

10. Environment

11. Culture

12. Arts

So, with this classification in mind it is clearer to see what we refer to when we talk about culture. And it is also evident that culture is overtly present in most course books as these are topics usually found in most of them

But still, what is its connection to CLIL?

What's CLIL?

"Content and Language Integrated Learning describes a pedagogic approach in which language and subject area content are learnt in combination. The generic term CLIL describes any learning activity where language is used as a tool to develop new learning from a subject area or theme." (Coyle, Holmes & King, 2009)

This is only one of multiple definitions of CLIL, but one that is simple and clear enough. CLIL as a term can be traced back to 1994 but its practice goes back to immersion education from as early as the 1970s. CLIL is especially strong in Europe, where it has been explicitly encouraged in official EU documentation since the 1990s.

Some of the benefits of CLIL are that it:

• builds **intercultural knowledge** and understanding

• develops **intercultural communication skills**

• improves language competence and oral communication skills

• develops multilingual interests and attitudes

• provides opportunities to study content through different perspectives

• diversifies methods and forms of classroom practice

• increases learners' motivation and confidence in both the language and the subject being taught

Here we can start to see its connection to culture.

4Cs curriculum

Coyle, Hood and Marsh (2010) illustrate CLIL with the following graph. It represents the 4Cs in the CLIL curriculum: Content, Communication, Cognition and Culture, where culture is the background where all the other aspects function. Culture is the necessary knowledge that binds all the other aspects together. And so we can say that cultural awareness is an essential part of CLIL.

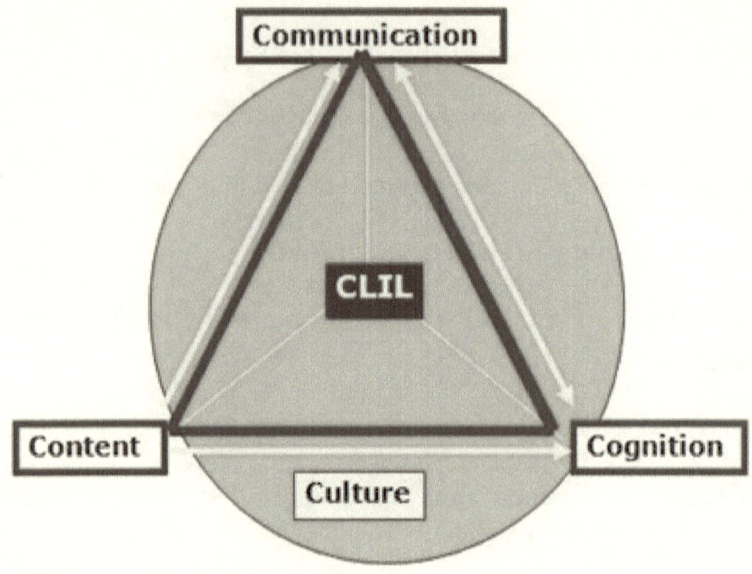

Figure 1: **4 Cs curriculum** (Coyle, Hood &Marsh, 2010)

As mentioned before, CLIL has been tried and tested, especially in Europe, and still there many different ways in which it can be implemented.

"Curriculum models for CLIL can vary in length from a single unit comprising a sequence of 2-3 lessons to a more sustained experience through modules lasting half a term or more. Some schools are developing bilingual sections where subjects are taught through the medium of another language for extensive periods." (Coyle, et al, 2009)

There are 3 main types or models of CLIL (Hawkes, 2010)

a) **'Integrated' or 'embedded' learning:** primary children practicing and/or using elements of the target language in a number of different contexts during the school week.

b) **Meanings that matter:** choosing engaging, age-appropriate topics as vehicles for language learning, drawing on content and/or activities used in other subjects, in some cases linking with work pupils are doing elsewhere.

c) **Bilingual or immersion learning:** teaching a subject in a way that involves learning another language, in addition to pupils having 'normal' language lessons.

In my personal teaching context, a regular secondary school in Argentina, I have experimented with the "Meanings that Matter" model, which I believe is a good starting point for language teachers who want to take advantage of CLIL benefits. And in this sense, and within this model, I have developed a series of steps that can be applied to any course book in order to give topics from course books a CLIL focus, taking into account the cultural aspect as well. It is simple to do if we go back to the 12 aspects of culture mentioned earlier, as these are topics commonly found in course books.

Giving topics from course books a CLIL focus

Step 1 Select a topic from the course book you are using. You can use the aspects of culture as a guide.

Step 2 Find a natural link between the material in the course book and real life.

Step 3 Find authentic material that supports your choice and ideas.

Step 4 Design a meaningful task to be done with the authentic material found.

Step 5 Provide necessary scaffolding during the task.

Examples

Food around the world

Step 1: Course book topic: Food.

Step 2: Link: What people eat around the world/ Healthy and unhealthy food and habits/ Relationship between food and geography.

Step 3: What the World Eats (Photo Essay) Time.

Step 4: Ask students to choose one of the pictures in the photo essay and do **oral presentations** where they can name the food they see, analyze healthy and unhealthy choices, compare with own typical diet, relate food to geography. Alternatively, they can prepare a presentation using a presentation tool, where they upload the pictures and they record themselves talking about them.

Another idea:

Step 3: What's in my Fridge today? Facebook group.

Figure 3. *What's in my fridge today?* Facebook group. Retrieved from https://www.facebook.com/WhatsInMyFridgeToday[1]

Step 3: Use these fridges' pictures to discuss different cultural/family food and eating habits. Have your students take pictures of their fridges and use them to discuss personal attitudes to food and eating.

Educational Systems

Step 1: Course book topic: Education.

Step 2: Link: Educational systems around the world.

Step 3: Google [2]Image search [3]for "Educational system".

---

1. https://www.facebook.com/WhatsInMyFridgeToday?hc_location=stream

2. https://www.google.com/

   search?q=japan+educational+system&hl=en&client=firefox-a&hs=XSW&rls=org.mozilla:es-ES:official&prmd=imvns&source=lnms&tbm=isch&ei=ifQAT8mDLcmEtgeky8TQBg&sa=X&oi=mode_link&ct=mode&cd=2&ved=0CB0Q_AUoAQ&biw=1680&bih=931

Step 4: Ask students to choose a country and make **posters** comparing that educational system with their own, regarding the levels, subjects, general organization, etc.

Note: Searching for images instead of websites can return very interesting infographics. Infographics are a meaningful way of presenting information to lower level students, who can then digest this information and express it in their own words.

Business Travel

Step 1: Course book topic: Business Travel.

Step 2: Link: Social customs around the world.

Step 3: Business etiquette websites (see references).

Step 4: Ask students to choose a country and **role play** situations in which they would have to act differently than in their own culture. In a multilingual/ multicultural class you can take advantage of students' knowledge of their own culture. Alternatively, they can record themselves using their mobile phones' cameras.

Travel Guides

Step 1: Course book topic: Travel Guides/ Tourism.

Step 2: Link: Travel guides or brochures.

Step 3: Travel websites or Travel guide creators such as Nile Guide (see references).

---

3. https://www.google.com/
search?q=japan+educational+system&hl=en&client=firefox-a&hs=XSW&rls=org.mozilla:es-
ES:official&prmd=imvns&source=lnms&tbm=isch&ei=ifQAT8mDLcmEtgeky8TQBg&sa=
X&oi=mode_link&ct=mode&cd=2&ved=0CB0Q_AUoAQ&biw=1680&bih=931

Step 4: Ask students to choose a country or their own country (in multicultural settings) and **design a travel brochure** with the main sights and landmarks. Set requirements to make the task more original and engaging, such as how much money you can spend, who are the travelers, what type of travelers they are (family, adventure, romantic), how long is the trip, etc. In a multilingual/ multicultural class you can have them prepare a travel brochure about their own country to tap into their background knowledge. The Nile Guide website offers the possibility of searching tourist locations and creating a personalized itinerary including landmarks, museums, hotels, restaurants, etc. that can be shown as a list and as a map over the trip period selected.

Step 5 Scaffolding Suggestions

• Ask students what they know about the topic to get them thinking and to activate their background schema.

• Pre-teach the necessary vocabulary through pictures, mind-maps, organized lists, etc.

• Monitor students` work and provide language/grammar support as needed, either individually or for the whole class. Be on the lookout for emergent language and step in to help students.

• Organize rehearsals for oral presentations and role plays. Sometimes, when we organize speaking activities, we do not give our students enough preparation time. We throw them in at the deep end and expect them to succeed.

• Suggest ways/strategies to optimize learning and organization. Each student is different and we should do learner training related to different ways of studying, recording vocabulary, etc. to help them find what works best for each.

Conclusions

If you are new to CLIL, this is an easy way to get you started basing your lessons and tasks on your own materials or course books. As you become more experienced, you can design longer, more extended tasks based on a topic of your choice. If you are more experienced in CLIL, you will hopefully have found some project ideas and tools that make the cultural aspect stand out. Any way, it is important to keep in mind the 4Cs of CLIL, content, communication, cognition and, especially, **culture**.

References

- Business etiquette links: (1) http://www.kwintessential.co.uk/resources/country-profiles.html, (2) http://www.cyborlink.com/

- Coyle, D., Holmes, B. &King, L. (2009) Towards an integrated curriculum – CLIL National Statement and Guidelines, The Languages Company.

- Coyle, D., Hood, P., Marsh, D. (2010) CLIL: Content and Language Integrated Learning

- Educational systems Google search https://www.google.com.ar/search?q=japan+educational+system&hl=en&client=firefox-a&hs=XSW

- Hawkes, R. (2010) CLIL Presentation. Retrieved from http://www.rachelhawkes.com/PandT/CLIL/CLIL.php

- Nile Guide http://www.nileguide.com/destination/la-paz-bolivia/things-to-do

- Time (2013) What the World Eats (Photo Essay). Retrieved from: http://time.com/8515/hungry-planet-what-the-world-eats/

- Twelve aspects of culture http://wiki.answers.com/Q/What_are_the_12_aspects_of_culture#ixzz1gMtBkM36[4].

- What's in my Fridge today? Facebook group https://www.facebook.com/WhatsInMyFridgeToday[5] was started by Carla Arena from Brazil and is a collaborative collection of pictures from teachers showing fridges from all around the world. In this article, she explains the project: http://collablogatorium.blogspot.com.ar/2012/06/facebook-collaborative-efforts-strikes.html

September 2013

Originally published in **ETAS Journal 2013 summer edition**

---

4. http://wiki.answers.com/Q/What_are_the_12_aspects_of_culture

5. https://www.facebook.com/WhatsInMyFridgeToday?hc_location=stream

Ways of promoting creativity in the classroom

As Einstein once said, *"Creativity is intelligence having fun"*. And as such I think creativity should be an important aspect of teaching and learning. However, it depends on us that creativity finds a place in our classrooms.

Some perceived barriers to creativity are routine, close-ended tasks, fear of being wrong or making mistakes, tight rules and the perception that fun is not conducive to learning. So varying what we do in the classroom, going for open-ended tasks, creating a safe environment for risk taking, having flexible rules according to aims and allowing for experimentation are some ways of creating an atmosphere where creativity can arise more easily.

Although my teaching background is mostly with teenagers, the ideas in this article can be used with all age groups. In my teaching practice, I have experimented with different ways of bringing my students' creativity to life. I have found different ways of stimulating creativity and these are some practical ideas that have worked for me:

Allow for open ended tasks so that students have room for choice

Choice is a natural partner of creativity. If you limit your students' work by providing stiff guidelines, it will be harder for creativity to arise. Open ended tasks in general and providing choices within tasks can deeply influence creativity from the very beginning.

Allow them to be exposed to different uses of language

Course books are generally filled with narrative and informative texts. Explore different genres and creative expressions. What about shape poems, haikus, classics with alternative endings, literal videos? You can then ask your students to try writing their own.

Here are some suggestions:

• *Word Whirls and other shape poems* collected by John Foster is a delightful collection of shape poems that can show students an alternative way of writing poetry.

• *Hairy Tales and Nursery Crimes* by Michael Rosen is a collection of well-known tales with alternative endings.

• *Wicked World* by Benjamin Zephaniah is a collection of poems on very interesting topics. You can also find videos of Benjamin Zephaniah himself reciting the poems.

• *The Melancholy Death of Oyster Boy and other stories* by Tim Burton is a fantastic collection of poems aligned with the film director's wacky style. There are also videos extending the stories in his poems.

• *Literal Harry Potter and the Deathly Hallows Trailer* is an example of alternative narrative in modern times. You can find it at http://www.youtube.com/watch?v=aVZNif6sd2s

Allow them to express who they are in different ways

Find new ways of doing the getting-to-know-you kind of activities. Let them talk about or show their interests and talents. For example, you can use Wordle to have your students create a word art poster about themselves and then use it in a variety of ways.

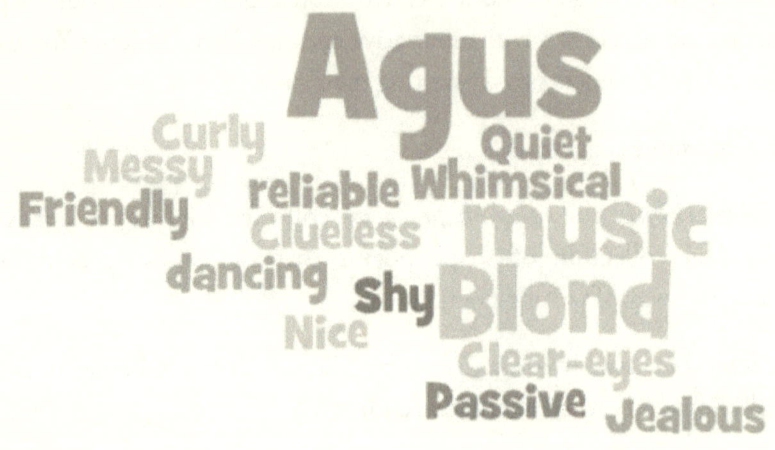

Another option is using Glogster for students to create interactive posters about themselves.

Allow them to become somebody else

Provide alternatives through creative writing, drama, digital storytelling. For example, you can ask them to research a time and place of their choice and then write a diary entry about a typical day in their life pretending they are somebody from that period. You will be amazed at who they choose to be: a samurai, a Native American, a Jew in Nazi Germany, a hippie, a Beatle-maniac, a 9-11 witness!

Allow them to explore literature in different ways

Let them choose how to respond to a reading. Promote new ways of doing book reports. For example, when we read an abridged version of *A Midsummer Night's Dream*, I suggested a list of possible options including making a video, writing character diaries, comparing different versions, doing character analysis, creating the stage setting and costume design, acting out a scene, among others. Here are some of my students' productions http://isfa.wikispaces.com/A+Midsummer+Night%C2%B4s+Dream

Conclusion

Promoting creativity in the classroom calls for an open-minded teacher. Think of different ways of doing the things you usually do. Be open to suggestions from your own students and guide them as to how they can achieve what they want to do. You will discover your students are a rich source of creative power that they can unleash under your mindful guidance.

References

• Burton, T. 1997. *The Melancholy Death of Oyster Boy & Other Stories*. New York: Harper Entertainment.

• Foster, J. (comp.) 1998. *Word Whirls and Other Shape Poems*. Oxford: Oxford University Press.

• Saumell, V. (2015) *Ways of promoting creativity in the classroom* in Pattinson, T. (Ed.). 2015. IATEFL 2014 Harrogate Conference Selections. Kent: IATEFL.

• Zephaniah, B. 2000. *Wicked World!* London: Puffin.

June 2015

Available online at http://www.teachingenglish.org.uk/blogs/vicky-saumell/vicky-saumell-ways-promoting-creativity-classroom

This article is based on a presentation given at IATEFL Harrogate 2014 and is also published in IATEFL 2014 Harrogate Conference Selections (2015)

Approaching literature with an open mind

I believe that using literature in a second language is a rich opportunity to see language in use. I have always tried to introduce authentic and graded literature in my classes with various degrees of success. Over the years, and with the belief that reading for pleasure is quite different from required reading, I have tried to lessen the negative effects of required reading.

Some strategies that have worked for me are:

Finding the right book or poem

This seems obvious but is an essential aspect of the process. I sometimes choose the reading myself, taking into account my students' age and preferences. Some other times I present them with a few options and they can vote which they want to read. Poetry is often seen as boring, but I believe this appreciation is related to the kind of poetry we present to our students. The poetry of Benjamin Zephaniah or Tim Burton are only two examples of a more accessible or different kind of poetry.

• *Wicked World* by Benjamin Zephaniah is a collection of poems on very interesting topics. You can also find videos of Benjamin Zephaniah himself reciting the poems.

• *The Melancholy Death of Oyster Boy and other stories* by Tim Burton is a fantastic collection of poems aligned with the film director's wacky style. There are also videos extending the stories in his poems.

Making sure the language level is accessible

A lower level might prove boring and a higher level will make it an unnecessary challenge. In this respect, nobody knows your learners better than yourself, so you will have to make this decision carefully.

Trying not to choke the pleasure of reading with excessive language work

Doing endless language exercises and comprehension questionnaires about the book you are reading can definitely make the reading tedious.

Allowing for a choice of reading response

Giving students a list of options for after reading projects is an effective way of allowing students some freedom to choose what they like best and to explore different aspects of the text. Students can then feel freer to explore their creative talents. One such list of options for A Midsummer Night's Dream is this:

A Midsummer Night's Dream

Reading Responses

Get into groups and choose what you want to work on from this list

- **Act out a scene**: Choose a scene (or portion) to present to the class. You may choose to rewrite your scenes or present them as they are.

- **Create a puppet show of a scene**

- Analyze **Shakespeare's language use** in the original play

- **Compare the three versions**: prose, cartoon, play

- **60 second Shakespeare**: create a 60-second video, slideshow, animation, rap or poem about the play

- Analyze **Shakespeare's time** at the time of this play

- **Character Diaries**: Choose a character and write a journal/diary from his/her point of view retelling all the events he/she experienced.

- A set of **comprehension activities** (worksheets)

- Create a **stage setting and costume design** for the play

- Create a **diagram of flow chart of the four pairs of lovers** – Theseus/Hippolyta, Oberon/Titania, Lysander/Hermia, and Demetrius/Helena – and explain how it changes throughout the play to the final pairings.

- Which of the four women is more like a **modern-day woman**? In what ways is each of them modern?

- **Character analysis**: choose one character and analyze it

- Write **Agony Aunt letters** from: Hermia, Helena and Egeus.

- Write or perform an **interview with a character**

- **Conflict resolution**: Hermia's father wants her to marry Demetrius. But she loves Lysander, and Lysander loves her. According to ancient laws without her father's approval, she can't marry him!!

What would happen nowadays in the same situation?

Why do young people in love sometimes experience conflict with their parents?

What is the best way to resolve a conflict?

If you have another idea, tell the teacher to see if it's possible

All in all, allowing students to enjoy what they are reading both because of the title selection and the work to be done has been a booster in my students' reaction to literature. I hope you can find ways to make it work for you!

February 2015

Available online at http://www.teachingenglish.org.uk/blogs/vicky-saumell/vicky-saumell-approaching-literature-open-mind

Turning homework into an effective learning opportunity

Homework is a complex issue with many factors affecting its success or failure. To begin with, homework is usually loaded with negative connotations. How can we turn homework into an effective language learning opportunity?

It is important to consider the teaching and learning context when we examine the homework issue:

• How many contact hours a week do these students have? Do they really need to extend exposure and practice beyond classroom time? How often?

• Are these students voluntarily attending English classes, or are these compulsory classes within their education system? What is their motivation to learn English?

• How much time do they have for homework assignments?

• Is homework your decision as a teacher or are you required to assign homework regularly?

• Is there a chance that students do not do the homework themselves?

• Are you going to check homework later? Will it be necessary the next class?

Here are a few considerations and suggestions:

• Make sure the homework is tied to what has been done in class. A clear connection as to why it's important to do this assignment is essential.

• Make sure the students can solve this task autonomously.

• Tasks that are not advisable to be done in the classroom should be best assigned as homework. Some of these tasks can be: writing tasks, personalised tasks, extensive reading tasks, research tasks, other tasks that take up too much time individually.

• Tasks that can easily be replicated or copied from another student are not good choices for homework.

• Tasks that need certain technology that you might not have available in the classroom are best assigned as homework: watching a video to be discussed later during class time.

• If you have to assign homework regularly, balance the type of homework and time needed to complete it. Long homework tasks are tedious...though sometimes necessary.

• Take advantage of technology to set up speaking homework: record yourself reading or speaking with a voice recording tool on mobile phones, record a video of your family as you explain who they are, record a video tour of your house.

• Flip the classroom. Have students watch videos about new topics, grammar explanations, discussion triggers, etc. Then you can use class time more effectively to discuss what they have watched.

• Assign personalised/differentiated tasks to address particular tricky areas for students.

• Assign listening homework! Let them choose a video to watch, something they are interested in, and have them report on what they watched the next class.

I am not very fond of homework unless it is really necessary. Above all I try to make homework fun!

July 2014

Available online at http://www.teachingenglish.org.uk/blogs/vicky-saumell/vicky-saumell-turning-homework-effective-learning-opportunity

Project-Based Learning as an alternative to coursebooks: an informal case study

Introduction

I have been a teacher for over 30 years and I have mostly taught with a course book. In the beginning of my career I taught with course books that were imposed on me by a higher authority or senior teacher who made such decisions. In time, I became that senior teacher myself and eventually the coordinator of my school so that course book selection was my responsibility. Indeed, I took it very seriously as I understood that the course book had a tremendous impact on learning. Together, of course, with the teacher!

I work in a school in Buenos Aires, Argentina, a private school with about 1,000 students at all levels, from kindergarten to secondary. Although it is private, it is far from the concept of a bilingual school. It is mostly funded by the state to keep the fees low and our students have only three hours of English instruction a week. This context influenced my selection process in that I needed a book that fitted my curriculum and my teaching beliefs and that was short enough to be covered in one school year and at a reasonable price.

So for about ten years, I tried to select the most appropriate course books for my context. I think I succeeded most of the times but not always...

However, something happened around 2008. I started feeling that students, especially teens, were not being offered the best option for their learning for a number of reasons:

• teachers were under pressure to use the whole course book because we had asked students to buy one and it was a big effort for most families. Therefore, there was no time to do other things, which were more creative or fun or relevant!

• the course books, however carefully chosen, did not fully reflect the students' interests and culture or the language we wanted them to learn or how we wanted them to learn.

• students were mostly unmotivated by the predictability of the course books.

• the occasional independent projects were welcomed with enthusiasm and offered a more creative output, which resulted in increased motivation for both the teachers and the students.

So I became quite restless and uncomfortable about this situation and I found myself asking the same questions again and again:

• What if we did away with course books altogether?

• What if we designed our own curriculum and materials?

• What if we introduced some kind of choice in the classroom?

• What if we tapped into our students' interests and knowledge to engage them in their own learning process?

• What if we started using web 2.0 technologies to break down classroom walls?

Yes! Why not? But there was no way I could do this on my own, so I approached one of my trusted teachers and told her that I was thinking about doing away with course books and writing our own materials instead, hoping to get any sign of approval. She said she thought that was really hard work, but she would do it!

So in 2009 I finally decided to make a dramatic change in the hope of really improving the quality of our students' learning.

The early years

The result was a new Project-Based Learning (PBL) scheme for grades 6 onwards, launched in March 2010, in which teachers design their own projects, taking into account the needs and interests of the students and the new syllabi, which had first been discussed and agreed on by all the teachers.

We found PBL was really appropriate for our context and our teaching beliefs, closely aligned with Constructivism, Connectivism, multi-literacies education for the 21st century, collaborative learning and the promotion of autonomous and lifelong learning.

A major concern was assessment: we discussed shifting from formal testing to continuous assessment through observation during the project development process and assessment of the final product.

We also held several meetings to discuss the necessary shift from a teacher-centered paradigm to a student-centered one, where the teacher would act as a facilitator. We envisioned the class as a place where students would feel the urge to speak the language, especially by providing real audiences by means of web 2.0 tools.

We created a wiki to be used as a project repository and as a record of which projects were done with which class. The wiki would also host resources related to project-based learning and technology integration, guides and tutorials for web 2.0 tools and any other material to support the scheme.

Three months into the new scheme we realized there was still a lot of work to be done: constant teacher support, periodic assessment of the project's development and analysis of problems to find solutions and improve the program.

But the overall feeling about the new PBL scheme was really positive. Teachers were excited about being able to do personalized and creative work. Here are some of their reactions.

"I can finally do drama activities."

"Working with songs they like is a great motivator."

"Being able to choose topics that they are interested in has resulted in more participation and eager production."

But what about the students? From their reactions, they seemed as excited about PBL as the teachers. They were motivated to work and really looked forward to their English lessons.

The importance of choice

Back in 1997, I first heard Andrew Littlejohn talking about choice in the classroom. At that time, I was using one of his course books, which included several instances of different options for students to choose about the same topic or task. From that moment on, I have seen how much students enjoy being given the possibility of choice! So we try to include different alternatives in every project we do, sometimes the choice refers to topic, sometimes the topic is fixed and they can choose the task to be done, sometimes the choice is in the way they want to work or the tools they can use. This is really motivating for teenagers because they can express their individuality through their choices and they feel they are being taken into account and respected. Choice also makes them more accountable for their own work.

The materials

Many schools photocopy materials from different course books to create a patchwork of materials. We don't think "patchworking" is the way to go about it. What we do is plan original projects using golden nuggets from the realm of authentic materials and then we build the project's scaffolding tasks, which occasionally include an activity from a photocopiable resource.

The costs

In terms of costs, the project based approach has not been a financial burden on the school itself. The school already had a computer lab with about 25 computers, which was only used by the Computer Studies teachers, and a beamer in another room, both of which we are now using regularly. The school has just bought one more projector. The photocopying costs, which are much lower than the cost of a textbook, are covered by the students. The only costs that we have asked the school to cover is the maintenance of the computer lab.

The wiki

The wiki is the PBL scheme backbone as it functions as a repository of all the projects so that they can be accessed by all teachers and be reused at will. There is a project index that includes the project name, their linguistic focus, level, age, when it was used and with which class. Then there is an individual page for each project where teachers upload the materials and lesson plans and can also leave comments on the projects they have done regarding suggestions, changes and challenges. Another part of the wiki is the web 2.0 tools guides, where I have built an index of web 2.0 tools with their uses, tutorials, guides, tips, etc., so that teachers can also develop professionally in this aspect.

The teachers' reactions

The teachers I coordinate have embraced this change. We used to have one bimonthly meeting that was not paid during the first two years of the project implementation. And I guess the reason why they always agreed to this is that the meetings were well planned and to the point. They did not extend beyond the agreed hour and a half unless they wished to stay a bit longer. The rest of the meetings were held during the period when there are no classes, except holidays, of course! As for their change of minds, we went through the hardest stage of the implementation scheme as they started to see beyond the expected advantages and notice some difficulties. The key to overcoming these difficulties was sharing them, suggesting solutions and providing continuous support to teachers. I have found that showing them my own difficulties and how I tackled them made the whole process more transparent. And acknowledging that this was a normal aspect of any change was reassuring for them.

Assessment considerations

Before the beginning of this project, we used to focus much more on grammar. Now we design the projects and the final products as a natural expression of the language, grammar and vocabulary we want them to learn and we provide grammar instruction and vocabulary development as needed during the projects, not before. The assessment is carried out through rubrics.

A rubric is a document that clearly states the expectations for an assignment, task or project by listing the criteria and levels of achievement or performance.

There are many types and styles of rubrics: from holistic to analytic, from general to specific. Most rubrics I have come across give equal weight to all the criteria included in the rubric, with 4 or 5 performance levels for each. This performance levels can be written as full descriptors for each or with generic descriptors for all, such as limited, developing, proficient, advanced, exemplary, or with numbers 1-5.

However, I think it is more effective to assign different levels of importance to the criteria so that, for example, language use is more important than deadline. To make this evident, from a total of 100 points, language use is scored out of 20 or 30 whereas deadline is scored out of 5 or 10. Thus, the perfect 100 points are divided into chunks of points for each criteria, where the most important ones carry more weight than the others. The rubric should be a transparent blueprint of the task or project to help students see and understand what aspects are essential and which are secondary.

We usually create two analytic rubrics for each project: a process one and a product one. During the development of the project (the process) we evaluate the students' performance in class through continuous observation. At the end of each project, we evaluate the final product, also according to a specially-designed rubric. The students have these rubrics from the beginning of the project. In some particular cases, if the teacher feels there is need for a specific grammar or vocabulary test, it is included as a third assessment instance for the project.

This allows us to focus on formative assessment while the students are working on the project, and then on summative assessment of the final product.

Creating your own rubric requires you to make a list of aspects you want to evaluate and then list them in order of importance and assign its individual score.

Some criteria that I might include in **process rubrics** are:

• Speaks English in class

- Speaks fluently

- Uses new vocabulary and structures

- Uses dictionary effectively

- Researches efficiently

- Reorganises information in his own words

- Solves problems creatively

- Brings materials

- Uses "...." tool effectively

- Works in class

- Participates actively

- Collaborates with group

Some criteria that I might include in **product rubrics** are:

- Written language use (vocabulary/grammar/register)

- Oral language use (fluency/pronunciation)

- Written/visual coherence

- Presentation/Design/Format

- Essay organisation

- Creativity

- Deadline

Here are a couple of examples to show how rubrics change depending on the project.

Art Stories

Name:

Date:

Aspects to be evaluated	Final Mark
Speaks English in class	/30
Speaks fluently	/10
Integrates structures	/10
Uses new vocabulary	/10
Participates actively and collaborates with group	/20
Uses dictionary efficiently	/10
Uses chosen tool effectively	/10
Total	**/100**

General oral language use	/30
General written language use	/30
Visual coherence	/15
Narrative concepts	/15
Deadline	/10
TOTAL	**/100**

Final mark and comment

HP Personal
Name:
Date:

Speaks English in class	/20
Uses new vocabulary	/15
Uses new structures	/15
Speaks fluently	/10
Brings materials	/10
Reorganizes information using own words	/10
Solves problems creatively	/10
Uses tools efficiently	/10
Total	**/100**

Written Language Use	/20
Oral Language Use	/20
Length (6 or +)	/10
Audio	/10
HP campaign similarity	/20
Creativity	/10
Deadline	/10
TOTAL	**/100**

Final mark and comment

My perceived benefits of using rubrics are these:

• They can teach students what is important to consider in each project, in terms of skills and content.

• They can guide students while working on the project itself.

- They can be used a checklist for students' self-assessment of their work prior to handing in their final products.

- They can help teachers when assessing projects by providing transparent aspects to consider.

Effective rubrics have to be well-designed, just as good tests. So writing good rubrics improves with practice!

Conclusion

The project is now in its 8th year and has become a part of our school identity. We have grown together, we have perfected the materials, the processes, the methodology, the assessment stages.

We have reused some projects over and over with minor adaptations. We have created lots of new projects every year to cater for our students' needs and interests. We have taken advantage of current affairs to develop projects. We have become comfortable teaching and learning in this way.

I feel happy now that I once questioned our habits, because it allowed me to develop professionally and to work for our students' benefit.

March 2017

Originally published in **EFL Talks ebook**

PART 3: Integrating Technology

Principles for Meaningful Technology Integration

Introduction

This article aims at analysing the complex issue of technology integration for language learning and developing a set of principles that can aid teachers in the decision-making process of integrating new technologies in different contexts, with a strong focus on pedagogical implications. It will include a brief description of existing models and seven principles outlined and analysed.

Existing models and perceptions

Some popular beliefs about technology integration that I have come across in my experience as a teacher and teacher trainer are:

- the need to have high-tech equipment,

- the need to have extensive technological knowledge,

- the need for constant updating,

- the need for extensive contact hours with the students to be able to obtain productive results.

These beliefs will be addressed by the article and I will come back to them in the conclusions.

Some existing models of standards for technology integration are the TPACK model by Mishra & Koehler (2006) and the SAMR model by Puentedura (2006), which look at technology integration from different perspectives.

The TPACK model developed by Mishra & Koehler looks at technology integration from a teacher's perspective. What are the different areas of knowledge a teacher must command in order to be able to integrate technology more effectively? The image below shows a triple Venn diagram showing that the 'hot spot' happens at the intersection of the technological knowledge, pedagogical knowledge and content knowledge. So for English language teachers, the ideal person to integrate technology into English language learning should be someone who knows English, who knows how to teach it and who knows about technology. This, in my opinion, has deep implications for English language teacher training programmes, which should include technology integration from the very beginning.

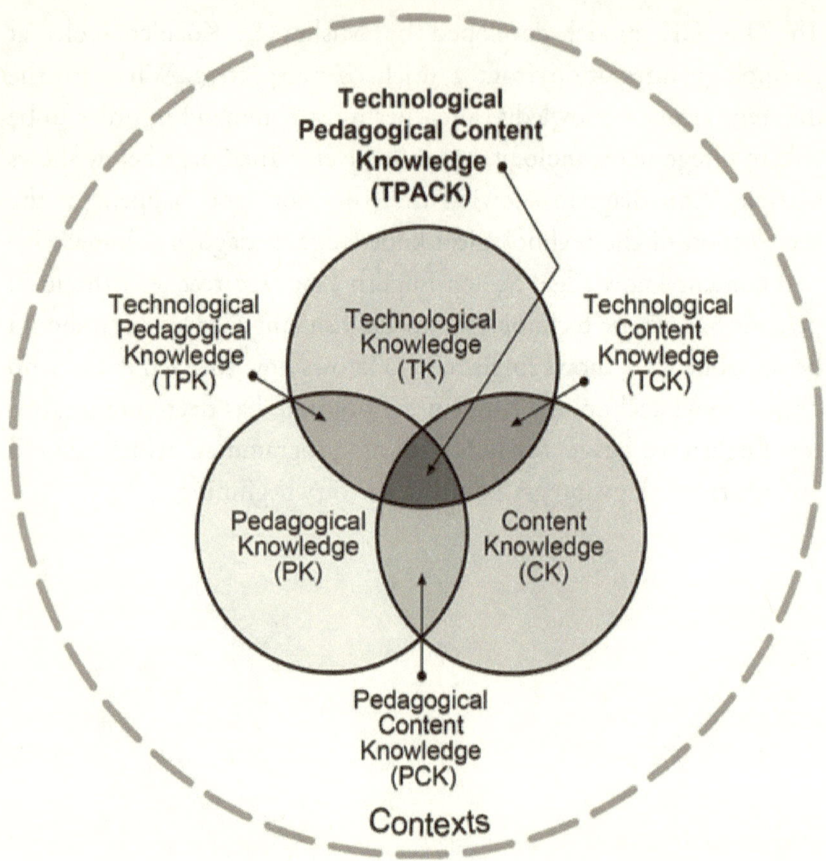

Image 1: TPACK model. Retrieved from http://tpack.org. Reproduced by permission of the publisher, © 2012 by tpack.org

A second model is SAMR by Ruben Puentedura. It looks at technology integration from the perspective of the tools used by both teachers and students. It analyses the way in which tech tools can be simple replacements of traditional procedures or whether they can enhance or transform the educational tasks.

He sees this model as a ladder, in which the first step is S for substitution, the second is A for augmentation, the third is M for modification and the last is R for redefinition.

In Substitution, tech acts as a direct tool substitute, with no functional change. In Augmentation, tech acts as a direct tool substitute but with some functional improvement. In Modification, tech allows for significant task redesign. And in Redefinition, the allows for the creation of new tasks, previously inconceivable.

He further describes the first two steps as an Enhancement phase and the last two steps as a Transformation phase.

There are multiple diagrams showing different tools and apps mapped out according to the SAMR model. A Google search will yield multiple results.

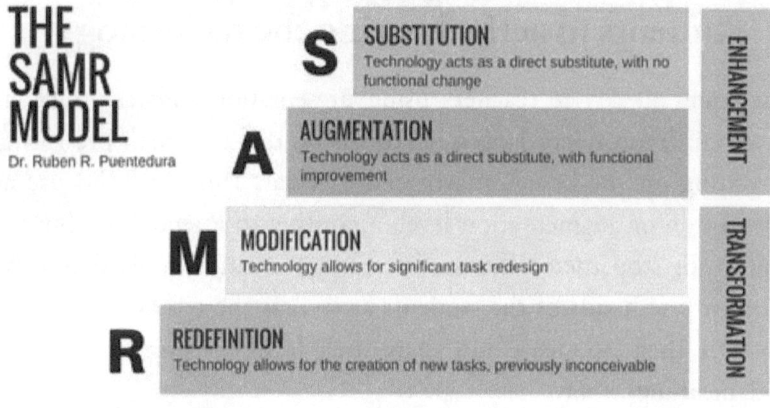

Image 2: SAMR model. Retrieved from Wikimedia Commons.

The understanding of these models has led me to the development of a set of principles and guidelines to aid teachers in the decision-making process of technology integration. This analysis focuses heavily on the pedagogical implications and knowledge needed for the process to be successful.

The Principles

Meaningful technology integration focuses on the learning task and not the technology

It sounds obvious but educational aims should always come first. What do you want to achieve? What are your aims and objectives, either in terms of language or skills? Is there a tool that will allow you to do it better, faster or more creatively than doing it in a traditional way? Other issues that I take into account are increased collaboration and meaningful use of language.

Meaningful technology integration involves the students in actively using the technology

It is common to see teachers using presentation software, such as Powerpoint, to present language. This is no different than presenting by writing on the board, maybe more visual. This is a valid use at substitution or augmentation level, according to Puentedura. But we should not stop there. The use of content creation tools should be placed in the hands of the students as well as the teachers. This will empower them to create and share their language productions in a more meaningful way.

Meaningful technology integration is essential not peripheral to the activity

Choosing a tech tool to dress up an activity is fine but we should strive for the use of tools which are essential to the activity. Why are we using this tool? Just because you can? Or because you can obtain more benefits doing it this way?

Meaningful technology integration works well for your specific context

Knowing your specific context is key to making appropriate decisions. Some context-related issues are:

- Are they working at school or from home?

- What connectivity quality do you have in your institution? And the students at home?

- Are you/your students using PCs or mobile devices?

- Are the mobile devices provided by the institution? Or do students bring and use their own mobile devices?

- If they will be using their own devices, what platform are they running on: IOS, Android or Windows?

All these questions will help to identify key information that you need in order to decide which tools to use and how, such as setting up the tasks to be done in class or as homework, deciding to have all students connected at the same time, choosing the most appropriate tools, choosing a multi-platform tool or alternative tools for different platforms to carry out a specific task.

Meaningful technology integration addresses 21st century skills´ issues and digital literacies training

Many teachers worry about the dangers of social media and online collaboration. There are indeed issues that need to be addressed if you are going to ´send´ your students online. This decision opens up the possibility of learning about being responsible and cautious digital citizens. It is a necessary challenge that we need to take up.

Some aspects that fall under the umbrella of digital literacies are:

- e-safety and privacy issues

- the ability to find and select information

- critical thinking and evaluation

- collaboration

- cultural and social understanding

Some teachers may think it is a waste of time to devote time and effort for this, but it is a much-needed part of education in general to teach our learners about digital literacies.

Meaningful technology integration facilitates learning activities that would be more difficult or impossible without the technology

This principle holds true in direct relationship with the SAMR model. One undeniable benefit of technology is that it allows us to do things that were previously unthinkable or impossible. We should therefore take advantage of this and choose tools that can take us beyond the traditional.

Some examples of tools that we can use are:

- Interactive posters creation with audio and video using Glogster or Thinglink.

- Digital storytelling tasks that combine text, images, audio and music using tools such as Powerpoint, Zimmer Twins, 30 Hands, Shadow Puppet or Adobe Voice.

- Multiple collaboration tasks using Google docs, Padlet or Voicethread.

- Speaking tasks with recording tools from mobile devices or Tellagami, Plotagon or Voki.

- Video creation with mobile devices or tools such as MailVu or the device's camera.

Meaningful technology integration breaks down classroom walls

Another undeniable benefit of technology is the possibility of easily connecting teachers, students, families and classes from all over the world. This possibility of becoming a connected classroom should not be disregarded.

Using tools to archive and share students' work is a powerful way of connecting with the community by creating a wider audience and of revisiting the students' productions for monitoring and assessment. Some tools that can help are blogs, wikis and social networking tools.

Using tools that promote collaboration can increase motivation by allowing us to set up twin class projects regardless of geographical location. Some useful starting points are Skype in the Classroom and ePals Global Community.

Conclusions

I have tried to show you existing research on models of technology integration and a set of straightforward principles to guide your practice. In doing so, I believe I have touched upon some of the initial perceptions mentioned:

• You can integrate technology effectively with as much or as little equipment as you have available.

• You do not need extensive technological knowledge but specific knowledge that you can apply in your particular context.

• The constant updating race is one you do not need to run. The really useful tools will be filtered through time and use by tech geeks who love to try and test every single new tool. Following a couple of language teachers who are experts on technology integration will do the trick. Social media is magic in this sense.

• You can achieve amazing results no matter how many contact hours you have with your students. I can attest to that!

I hope you now have a clearer picture of how this technology integration process can happen effectively in different contexts and you can put it in practice little by little.

References

• Mc Collum, K. Principles of effective technology integration. Retrieved July 2017: http://www.slideshare.net/kamccollum/principles-of-effective-technology-integration-presentation

• Mishra, P. & Koehler, M. (2006). Technological pedagogical content knowledge: A framework for teacher knowledge. *Teachers College Record*. Retrieved July 2017: http://one2oneheights.pbworks.com/f/MISHRA_PUNYA.pdf.

• Puentedura, R. (2006) *Transformation, Technology, and Education*. Retrieved July 2017: http://www.hippasus.com/rrpweblog/archives/2014/06/29/LearningTechnologySAMRModel.pdf[1]

---

1. http://www.hippasus.com/rrpweblog/archives/2014/06/29/
LearningTechnologySAMRModel.pdf%20

February 2016

Originally published in **Modern English Teacher April 2016**

Key Considerations for Technology Integration in the Young Learner Classroom

Although technology influences many aspects of our lives, many teachers often feel apprehensive about integrating technology in the young learner classroom. This article aims to outline some key considerations for a meaningful and effective use of technology with learners aged between four and ten.

Assess context

Context is the single most important consideration. A careful look at your school and your class is the first step.

What technology is available at your school? Is internet access easy, and are there laptops or mobile devices for students to use? What's the school's attitude to using technology in the classroom? Is integrating technology popular and expected? Is it even compulsory? Or is it rare and even disapproved of? Are you introducing technology in the classroom for the first time or are there already institutional policies in place? If you want to introduce it, make use of existing projects as examples to convince the school of what is to be gained from integrating technology. In this wiki, by Shelly Sanchez Terrell and Ozge Karaoglu, you will find lots of examples http://technology4kids.pbworks.com/w/page/24292734/FrontPage.

Regarding your class, assessing your learners' language ability, age, interests and, of course, your learning aims, is essential. Nobody knows the learners better than their teacher. You will know what can work and what cannot. Bear in mind that often, young learners have a fantastic grasp of technology, and may even be able to show you how to work devices or explain how things work. Make use of this knowledge and allow them to take control of their learning, where appropriate.

Identify educational aims

Whatever technology you decide to use, it should help you and your learners achieve a learning goal. Integrating technology does not mean you have to do it every class, even if you have the technology available. How can technology enable you to do something better or in a different or more creative way? Oral work to develop speaking skills used to be constraint to classroom work, but technology has enabled the recording of our learners' speech so that we can now think of new ways of doing speaking tasks, for example, at home. If it is just a replacement, you may wonder whether it is worth at all. For example, reading a text online may just replace reading one in a book, but it is the added content that makes using e-books worthwhile, e.g. audio, video clips and games.

Choose the right technology

Once you have identified the available technology in your school consider what technology the learners have at home. Do they use devices on their own or with their families' help or supervision?

Will you be using PCs or mobile devices? How many will you have available? This will have an impact on the task dynamics. A class set of tablets or PCs or learners bringing in their own devices will allow you to do individual work. With fewer devices, you can still do group activities. If there is only one PC or mobile device available, you can do whole-class activities or rotating group tasks by creating stations. Stations are different spaces in the classroom where students have to do different tasks, with different materials. You can have paper-based stations or digital stations, with the devices available. The class is divided into as many groups as there are stations and after a set time, they rotate to the next station to perform a different task.

If you have mobile devices available, do they operate on Android or iOS? Choosing a tool that runs on all platforms, including PCs, is a wise decision. There are many tools that meet this need. However, you can also identify the type of task you want to do and select different tools with similar functions according to platform. For example, Fotobabble is a tool that allows you to add audio to a photograph, but it only works on iOS. A similar tool for Android phones is Talking Photos.

Keep it simple

Choose simplicity. Go for easy to use tools. Generally speaking, if learning how to use the tool takes longer than the activity you plan to do with it, you may want to reconsider.

Another consideration is the login process. Try to go for no-login tools so that you or your learners do not need to create an account to use them. If you have to, assign passwords to your learners following a clear logic, such as your initials_class_list number (e.g. AF_4a_22). Remind learners not to tell anyone their password and not to log in using anyone else's details.

Choose versatility

Go for a few versatile tools that you can use again and again. There are many tools that can be used for different types of tasks. An interesting starting set of tools could be:

• an audio recording tool (e.g.Vocaroo, Fotobabble or Tellagami)

• a tool to work with images (e.g. Skitch or PicCollage)

• a tool to work with words (e.g. Wordle or Word Salad)

• a tool to create presentations (e.g. Shadow Puppet or Storyrobe) or videos.

Start with your favourite and once your learners have learnt how to use it, add a new one. Do not overload them or yourself with new tools.

Consider e-safety issues

The main concern in the young learner classroom is e-safety. If you intend to share the learners' work online, either by posting to a website or blog or by sharing through social media, you may want to avoid using the learners' own images. Using the learners' voices or creating avatars instead of using their photos is an alternative. This may seem like a constraint, but there are multiple options for tasks that do not require the learners' images. Also, working with apps instead of the World Wide Web is safer since we will avoid YLs accessing inappropriate content. It is important to monitor their work and to instruct learners to tell you if they find anything upsetting and unsuitable. Learners should also be advised to keep all personal info private. For very young learners, the sharing process should be carried out by the teacher, not the learners.

You should ask parents/carers to sign a Consent Form giving authorisation for their children to access the Internet as part of their English class, and permission for their child's photo/image, work and videos to be shared online.

Engage families

Parents' opinions on technology integration in their children's education is very important and you will want to have families on board. You could have a meeting with parents and explain why you want to use technology and what you expect to gain or send them a letter or email explaining this. Show examples of work done by students and mention the benefits, such as collaborating with other classes, creating content, being active participants. Be clear about the importance of families' support in this process, as some tasks may have to be done at home in collaboration with parents. Mention the Consent Form if you intend to share their work online, and ask them to sign and return it.

Make it fun

Technology in itself is usually a motivator. Find ways of having students show you how they can use the language in fun, creative ways. For example, creating speaking avatars for characters in a book they read, or creating a word art poster about themselves. Choice can be a great ally. Allow for some aspects of the task to be chosen, the topic or the tool, or which character to talk about, and create a relaxed atmosphere where creativity can arise. A task that is too rigid will stifle creativity. You will want your young learners to enjoy the tasks as much as possible.

Once you get started on this journey, keep a journal of your experiences to record your successes and your failures, things that worked well, things that can be adapted and improved, things that did not work at all. So be reflective, but do not be afraid to try new things. Young learners are very enthusiastic, at ease with technology and will welcome your ideas!

Further reading

• My First Digital Journey e-book by Özge Karaoğlu & Jennifer Verschoor

• Tech it Easy with Very Young Learners blog post by <u>Özge Karaoğlu</u> http://ozgekaraoglu.edublogs.org/2010/06/01/tech-it-easy-with-very-young-learners/.

• Technology for Kids wiki by Shelly Sanchez Terrell and <u>Özge Karaoğlu</u> http://technology4kids.pbworks.com/w/page/24292734/FrontPage.

• Using Technology with Young Learners webinar by Sedef Cok http://www.cambridge.org/elt/blog/2014/03/using-technology-young-learners/.

December 2014

Originally published on the **Cambridge English Teacher website**

Essential Digital Toolbox for Primary Teachers

Initial questions

Using digital technology tools in the primary classroom can raise a few concerns but has a lot of potential if considered thoughtfully. A good starting point is thinking about the following:

What is a set of useful tasks for the primary classroom? That is, what kind of tasks do we usually do in a primary language learning setting?

What can technology allow you to do? And how?

It should be clear at this point that we always start from a pedagogic point of view, the learning objectives. By focusing first on our educational aims, we can then start thinking about the technological affordances and constraints. That is, how can technology help us to do something and how can it complicate or hinder our actions?

A list of such useful tasks could be:

- Manipulating materials

- Working with images

- Working with words

- Working with speech

These are common tasks in a language classroom. Now, how can technology allow me to do these tasks better or in a different way?

This is the same list of tasks, now expressed through a technological lens:

- Digitalising materials

- Working with digital images

- Working with words

- Recording learners' speech

- Creating videos

These are tasks that we can do even with little technological equipment or support. The technological support available will determine different implementation strategies. Still, these tasks are definitely possible in low-tech contexts.

The next step is: what is a basic list of equipment necessary?

- An internet connection

- A PC or laptop or mobile device, such as a tablet or mobile phone

- A webcam and a microphone, either separate or built-in

In the case of PCs, you will need an external webcam and microphone. In the case of laptops and mobile devices, these are built-in.

Having set the initial mindset and equipment necessary, we will now focus on the tasks and suggest some tools and examples.

Digitalising materials

Before we can even start to work with digital images, we need to think about the possibility and potential of generating our own digital images. Work in the classroom has long been based on what is done on paper or on the board. Whether it is an interesting image or text from a book, a drawing or piece of work done by the learners on paper, or the learners' or teacher's work on the board, it can easily be digitalised by taking a picture of it. Once it is digitalised, there are multiple things we can do with it: project it with a beamer, manipulate it with another tool, share it with others, etc.

Working with images

Language teachers have used images in a variety of ways for a long time. Flashcards and posters are popular and they lend themselves to many different types of tasks. There are many digital tools that allow us to work with digital images in similar ways and in new ones.

Skitch is a free application that runs on PCs, both Windows and Mac, and on mobile devices, both Android and IOS. It allows you to upload a digital image and then manipulate it or add text, which you can then move around by dragging.

Some ideas for using Skitch are:

• Taking a picture from your coursebook or a drawing made by the learners and project it to use as a prompt for a class activity.

• Adding text to the uploaded image: labelling vocabulary, describing the picture, etc.

• Jumbling words and having learners match words and pictures.

Example 1:

A family drawing by a learner has been uploaded. The names and family relations have been added. Learners have to match names and relations by dragging and dropping. Learners can draw their own family and create their individual family posters.

Figure 1: An example using Skitch

PicCollage is another free application that runs on Android and IOS mobile devices. It allows you to upload one or multiple pictures to create a collage and add text. You can re-arrange the pics and the words by dragging and dropping.

Some ideas for using PicCollage are:

• Uploading pics and having students re arrange them in a logical way

• Uploading pics related to a lexical set and creating a picture dictionary

These collages can also be printed as posters to decorate the classroom or shared online with learners and their families, or with an even wider audience.

Example 1:

Separate pictures of family members retrieved from a coursebook have been uploaded. Arrows have been added. Learners have to re arrange the pics to create a family tree. Alternatively, learners can create their own family trees with their own pictures.

Figure 2: A family tree task using PicCollage

Example 2:

A shops picture dictionary with photos taken by the learners

Figure 3: A picture dictionary using PicCollage

Working with words

Learning languages is obviously related to working with words. Technology has made it possible to work with words in novel ways.

Wordle is a free web-based service that allows you create word art posters from a given text or list of words. Wordle analyses the words frequency and displays the words in different sizes according to their frequency within the text or list.

Some ideas for using Wordle are:

• Displaying lexical sets from a vocabulary list

• Displaying collocations

• Displaying a text's main ideas

The word posters can then be exploited in different ways:

• As a prompt for oral/written work

• To classify vocabulary into categories

• To show hierarchy within a group of words

• To show a text's main ideas

• To recognise words that collocate

Example 1:

From a list of animals, learners can classify into categories: mammals, reptiles, etc.; according to what they eat or where they live, according to body parts, according to size, etc.

Figure 4: A Wordle with animals

Example 2:

From a list of prepositions of time and time words, learners can make a list of words that collocate with each preposition.

Figure 5: A Wordle about prepositions of time

Word Salad is a similar app that runs on IOS and Android mobile devices. They main difference is that it does not analyse word frequency. The free version has a watermark in the background but is fully functional.

Recording learners' speech

Oral work in language learning has been confined to face to face interactions in the classroom. However, technology has made it easy to record learners´ speech.

The benefits of using voice recording tools are:

• Teachers can assign oral homework

• Teachers can assess oral work at home

• Teachers and learners can add oral artifacts to e-portfolios

• Teachers and learners can record learners´ oral proficiency at any given time to be revisited later to monitor progress

• The learners can record and re-record as many times as they want until they are satisfied with the result. This process implies more repetition and practice

• The learners' own images are not used so these recordings or artifacts can be shared and uploaded to a website without having to worry about e-safety issues, especially connected with young learners

• Learners who are shy or lack confidence may prefer not to appear on camera, or to 'hide' behind an avatar, thus making voice recording an encouraging option

Vocaroo is a very simple free web-based tool that allows you to record your voice and then send it by email, download it, post it to a website or share it through social media.

Tellagami is a free app that runs on Android and IOS mobile devices. It allows you to create an avatar (a digital representation of a person) and then record your voice to make the avatar 'speak'.

Fotobabble is a free app for IOS and Android mobile devices but it is also web-based so you can use it from a PC or laptop. It allows you to upload an image and then record a message to go with it.

Figure 6: An example of how Tellagami looks

Some ideas for using these recording tools are:

• Having learners record themselves reading aloud or saying chants or tongue twisters

• Having learners create an avatar for themselves and record their personal introductions

• Having learners create an avatar for a specific situation or character and record what they would say

• Have learners upload a picture and describe it or give an opinion. This is particularly useful for exam classes requiring a picture description task in the oral examination.

Creating videos

If there is one thing that technology has enabled, it is the possibility of creating videos. What was once only possible through specialized and expensive equipment, today is an easy and practical reality as most mobile phones have video recording capabilities. Videos can be used in a variety of ways but their main advantage is putting learners in the position of content creators to develop meaningful language tasks.

MailVu is a free web-based service and app for Android and IOS that allows you to record a short video (10 minutes) and send it directly by email.

Some ideas for using MailVu (or the mobile device camera directly) are:

• Introducing their families by recording them at home

• Showing their bedroom and what is in it

• Showing their clothes and describing them

• Showing their house, or school, or neighbourhood, like a tour.

• Recording themselves doing a role play or interview.

Tools	Platform	Cost	Description
Fotobabble	Web based/IOS	free	Talking pictures
Mailvu	Web based/IOS/Android	free on mobile $2.50 on PC	Video emails
Pic collage	IOS/Android	free	Digital posters.
Skitch	Web based/IOS/Android	free	Digital posters
Tellagami	IOS/Android	free	Speaking avatars
Vocaroo	Web based	free	Very simple audio recording, no registration required
Wordle	Web based	free	Word clouds
Wordsalad	IOS/Android	Free (with watermark)	Word clouds

Figure 7: A summary of the tools

Final considerations

After having read about the many possibilities outlined in this article, you may still be wondering which to choose and where and how to start. As I mentioned before, any use of technology must come from the understanding that it will help you achieve a goal. In terms of which tool to choose, it is important to examine your specific context, your institution and your learners.

Some questions that might help are:

• What technology is available at my institution? Is there a computer lab, or a PC in each classroom? Is there a set of tablets? Is there an internet connection?

• What technology is available at your learners' homes? Do they have a PC, or a mobile device?

• If they have a mobile device, do they bring it to school? What type of mobile devices do they have? Are they all IOS, or Android, or mixed?

The answer to these questions will guide you in selecting the right tool. I have made sure there are tools for PCs and for mobile devices alike, and both for IOS and Android. Then, whether learners bring their own devices or there is a set of PCs or tablets, or just one or two per class, all the ideas presented can be carried out with minor adjustments, either individually, in groups or as a whole class.

Also, if you are taking your first steps with technology, choose the one activity that attracted you the most and try it. A versatile tool can be used for many different purposes and activities. Think of other ways of using the same tool so that you do not have to teach learners how to use many different tools. Keep it simple and add a new tool when learners are confident using the first. Do not overload them or yourself! As with everything in life, practice makes perfect! Are you ready to start?

References

• Saumell, V. (2014) Essential Primary Digital Toolbox webinar. Available online at http://www.cambridge.org/elt/blog/2014/10/ essential-digital-toolbox-primary-teachers/.

November 2014

Originally published in **Modern English Teacher January 2015**

Digital Storytelling

As a teacher, I have always endorsed the use of creative writing as an enjoyable way of developing writing skills. As a firm advocate of meaningful technology integration to develop language skills, I have found digital storytelling to be a great way of blending the writing with the audiovisual in a creative way.

Digital Storytelling is any combination of images, text, audio and music to create a digital story, either fictional or non-fictional.

I have worked on different ways of implementing digital storytelling with teens. And from my experience these are what I believe to be its benefits.

• It is student-centered and therefore lends itself to more personalized tasks.

• You can set it up in such a way to promote collaboration among learners, either by assigning roles such as writer, spell checker, image editor, voice over narrator, or by having students reaching consensus and working together towards a common goal.

• It definitely stretches their creativity and thinking skills.

• It is a fantastic way of working with digital literacies in terms of image copyright for example. You can introduce Google Images advance search options and Creative Commons Licenses.

• It is a great way of connecting the original writing with speaking. I usually have my students doing voice over narration instead of adding subtitles.

• Last but not least, it is fun and it genuinely motivates students!

I have experimented with many tools, whether pc-based, web-based or mobile apps. Most of the tools are for use online (digital storytelling) but others can be used in the classroom to support pen and paper storytelling.

I usually start with traditional pen and paper storytelling. I work with my student in a process writing approach and discuss strategies to improve their stories, depending on the genre we are tackling. Only when they feel satisfied with their written stories we move to the digital aspect of storytelling: adding images and audio. Alternatively, you can start with the images as a trigger for the story writing. However, you can also go for using tools which support traditional storytelling in the classroom. My suggestion is to start small with a task and tool you feel comfortable with and then increase the complexity little by little.

These are some digital storytelling tools you can use. There is a wide variety to cater for different aspects of storytelling, some are more visual, others rely more on the story. Some are very simple to use and others are more complicated. Take your pick and bring storytelling to life in your classroom!

To support storytelling in the classroom

Flickr Tell a story in 5 frames

Sets of 5 images that make up a story. Assign a set or have your students choose one and write the story.

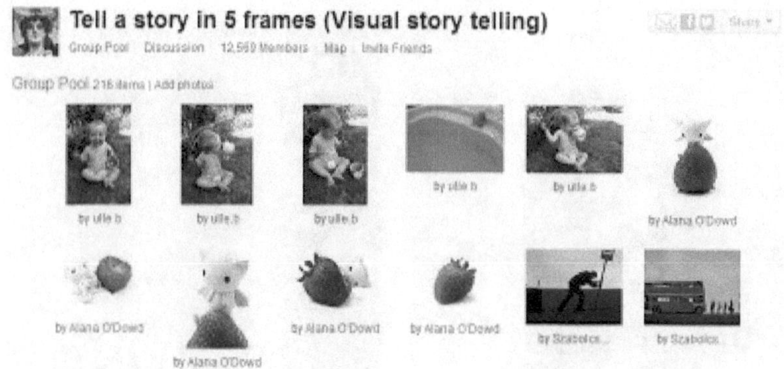

Figure 1: Flicker Tell a Story in 5 frames

Story Starter Jr

Random creator of story starters

Rory's Story Cubes $1.99 for iPhone and iPad/ $1.93 for Android

Dice with images. Simply shake your iPhone to roll the cubes and create a story using all 9 face-up images. Thanks to Graham Stanley for this one!

Figure 2: Rory's Storycubes screenshot

Story Dice $1.99 for iPhone and iPad

Story Dice is a creative tool to prompt ideas for plot, character, and setting. This idea generator can be used effectively for both written and oral storytelling.

Figure 3: Story Dice screenshot

Tell a tale Free for iPad

You'll get the first and the last sentence of a story, three pictures are added and the rest is up to you.

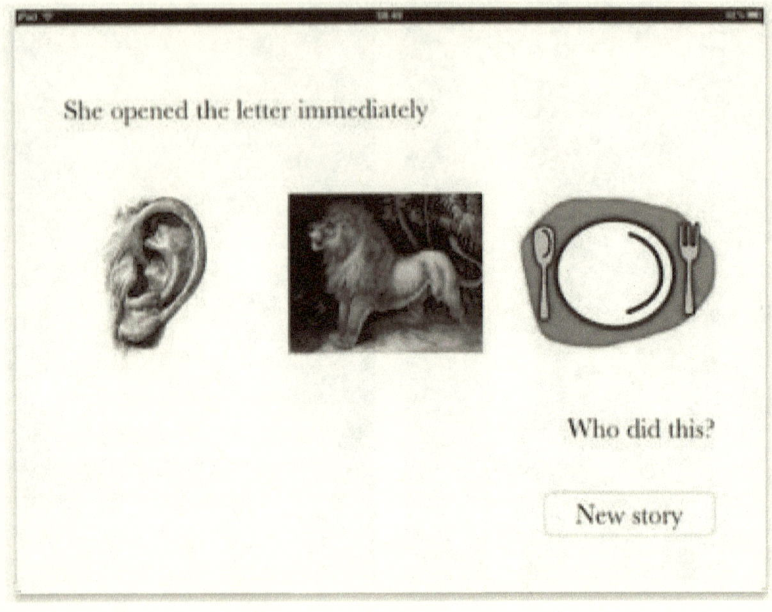

Figure 4: Tell a Tale screenshot

Writer's Hat $0.99 for iPhone and iPad

Writer's Hat is an ideas generator to inspire creative writing, oral literacy and imaginative thinking.

Figure 5: Writer's Hat screenshot

PC-based tools

Powerpoint and **Windows Movie Maker** allow you to combine images, text, music and audio to create digital stories without the need of an Internet connection.

Web-based tools and apps (to be used online)

Animoto[1] allows you to upload images and combines them automatically with a selection of background music available on the website. The free version has a 30 seconds limit. For longer videos, you need the paid version.

Xtranormal[2] allows you to create text to speech animations.

---

1. http://animoto.com/

Voicethread[3] is a slide show creator, in which you can type or record comments around each slide. It is also available for iPad and iPhone.

Zimmer Twins[4] is an animation creator, where you can choose from 3 characters (a boy, a girl and a cat) but you can then customize their actions, face expressions, verbal utterances, background, objects in their hands and transitions. It is very versatile and it automatically adds sound effects according to your choices. This is one of my favourites!

Figure 6: Zimmer Twins screenshot

Pixton[5] is a complex comic creator tool where you can choose a template and customize it, or you can start from scratch. The final result looks very professional!

---

2. http://www.xtranormal.com/

3. http://voicethread.com/

4. http://zimmertwins.com/

5. http://www.pixton.com/

Figure 7: Pixton screenshot

Storybird[6] is a digital storybook creator. You choose the illustrations you can to include in your story from what is available in the website. There is a huge collection of beautiful illustrations by amazing artists. You can search by artist or theme/keyword. You can then add text below the illustrations. The result is absolutely fantastic!

<hr>

6. http://storybird.com/

Figure 8: Storybird screenshot

Figure 9: Storybird screenshot

Pic Lits[7]

I love Pic Lits. You can read my previous blog post[8] on it for more details.

---

7. http://www.piclits.com/compose_dragdrop.aspx

8. http://educationaltechnologyinelt.blogspot.com.ar/2009/02/piclits.html

Figure 10: PicLits screenshot

Folding Story[9]

Folding Story is a web game in which players write one line of a story, fold the paper, and pass it on to the next person.

---

9. http://foldingstory.com/

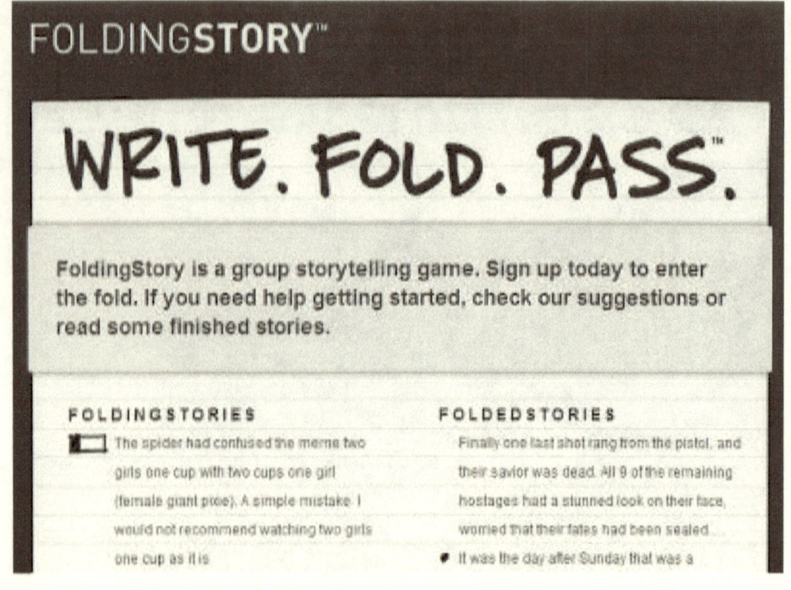

Figure 11: Folding Story screenshot

Story wheel $2.99 for iPhone and iPad

1-4 players can create a story. Start by spinning the wheel to get a picture. Next, record your voice as you develop a story with that picture. Each player will build upon the story with a new picture. When done, you can listen to your story and share your creations online, or email them to family and friends.

Figure 12: Storywheel screenshot

Story Patch $4.49 for iPad

Story Patch is a new application for the iPad that children can use to create their own picture books. With hundreds of included images, easy-to-use controls, and the ability to import photos.

Figure 13: Story Patch screenshot

Storyrobe $0.99 for iPhone and iPad

This is a really great app for making photo slide shows with voice recording.

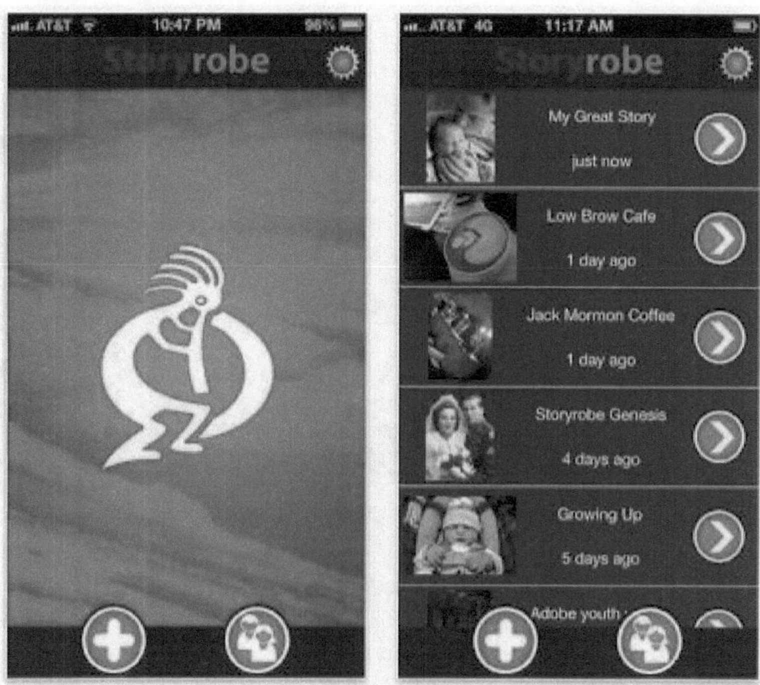

Figure 14: Storyrobe screenshot

Tellagami Free for iPhone and iPad

Tellagami is a quick and easy way to create and share a fun short story called a Gami. Just select and customize a character. Personalize your Gami with photos and your own voice. Then share your Gami with friends.

Figure 15: Tellagami screenshot

ThumbStruck Free for iPhone and iPad

Thumbstruck is a social networking/ storytelling application that allows users to improvisationally write stories together through three methods of interaction: Choose my words, Use my words, and Fuse my words.

Figure 16: Thumbstruck screenshot

To see three examples of digital storytelling projects I did with my students from **Instituto San Francisco de Asis** in Buenos Aires, Argentina, you can see my presentation at **IATEFL Glasgow 2012** for the Technology and Teens Symposium organised by Graham Stanley. Here are the slides for my presentation **Implementing Digital Storytelling with Teens**[10]

Hope you have found something to spice up your storytelling activities!

March 2013

Originally published in **Etas Journal 2013 Fall edition**

---

10. http://www.slideshare.net/vickys16/implementing-digital-storytelling-with-teens

About me

I hold a degree in Spanish-English Literary and Technical Translation, a Diploma in the Theory and Methodology of TESOL and a Postgraduate Degree in Educational Technology.

I am the Overall Coordinator of the EFL department at Instituto San Francisco de Asís, a private school in Buenos Aires, Argentina, where I have worked for 25 years.

I was the author and tutor of *New Learning Environments* for the Master's in ELT at Universidad de La Sabana, Colombia, where I taught online from 2009 to 2014.

I am co-author of *Teacher Development Interactive: Preparing for the Teaching Knowledge Test (TKT)*[1], author of *Meeting Point 3*[2] *and 4* for the Storyline coursebook series and series consultant for *English in Common*[3] coursebook series, all for Pearson. I have written online

1. *http://www.teacherdevelopmentinteractivetdi.com/pdf/TDI_Brochure_Pager_Press_National.pdf*

2. *http://www.pearsonlongman.com.ar/catalogue2011/download/STL/STL_meeting_3.pdf*

teacher training courses on digital tools and digital materials for *Eyes Open* and *Uncover* coursebook series, all for CUP.

I have been doing volunteer work with IATEFL since 2013. I am currently a committee member of both IATEFL Learning Technologies SIG and Publications Committee.

I am also a freelance materials writer, teacher trainer and presenter at professional development conferences, especially on the integration of new technologies for language learning.

Feel free to contact me!

Email vicky.s@umell.com.ar

Website http://vickysaumell.com

Twitter @vickysaumell

Facebook https://www.facebook.com/vicky.saumell

LinkedIn https://www.linkedin.com/in/vickysaumell/

---

3. *http://www.pearsonelt.com/englishincommon/?WT.mc_id=EICtop*

My publications

Co-author of *Teacher Development Interactive: Preparing for the Teaching Knowledge Test (TKT)*[1] (Pearson) 2009

---

1. *http://www.teacherdevelopmentinteractivetdi.com/pdf/*

TDI_Brochure_Pager_Press_National.pdf

Author of ***Meeting Point 3***[2] ***and 4*** for the Storyline coursebook series (Pearson) 2010

 VICKY SAUMELL

Series consultant for ***English in Common***[3] coursebook series (Pearson).

---

3. *http://www.pearsonelt.com/englishincommon/?WT.mc_id=EICtop*

Author of ***Ways of promoting creativity in the classroom*** in IATEFL 2014 Harrogate Conference Selections (IATEFL)

 VICKY SAUMELL

Author of Digital materials for *Eyes Open* and *Uncover* coursebook series (CUP).2015

Technology Consultant for ***Kid's Box*** coursebook series (CUP)

Author of ***Digital Storytelling as an Effective Language Learning Task*** in Teaching English Reflectively with Technology (IATEFL LT SIG and TESOL CALL-IS) 2017

www.ingramcontent.com/pod-product-compliance
Lightning Source LLC
Chambersburg PA
CBHW020731160726

47993CB00006B/2412